abc of

COMMERC

by DAVID J. WARBURTON

LONDON :

Ian Allan Ltd

INTRODUCTION

EVERY two years, the Society of Motor Manufacturers and Traders holds its Commercial Motor Exhibition at Earl's Court, London. Of late, the interest shown in this Show by ordinary people not connected with the industry in any way has been such as to make the preparation of this booklet an almost imperative task. It is gratifying to think than an important cause of this rising interest is almost certainly a sense of pride in the achievements of the British Motor Industry in world markets since the war, and perhaps the greatest of these have been won by our Commercial Vehicle Manufacturers, who have risen rapidly from a position of comparative obscurity in the international field to one of acknowledged supremacy.

Such is the extent of the unbroken range to be covered in this book, from the humble but spritely 5 cwt. vans to the roaring 100-ton tractors, that I have only been able to touch on each model, with basic dimensions to indicate power and size for those who like making comparisons. Power has been indicated in each case by the maximum brake horse-power developed, this unit having been chosen as the most accurate available for easy comparison.

Commercial users' requirements are so infinitely varied, that the industry can never hope to standardize its commercial products to the extent that mass-production has achieved for private cars. Some factories have simplified their processes by standardizing types in most popular demand, but others continue to cater for customers' special requirements, with skilled work of which they are rightly proud.

Practically all the companies whose products are described in the following pages (and all the principal makers are included) market their chassis as units ready for independent body-making. In fact, some especially passenger chassis builders such as Bristol and Daimler, do not build bodywork at all. In a book of this size it has only been possible briefly to mention

2

the range of chassis for each manufacturer, with a note of the key dimension of the standard type of body normally fitted to each wheelbase. To a great extent, these dimensions are governed not by the strength of the chassis or the power of the engine, but by Ministry of Transport regulations, which strictly limit the loads, seating capacities, lengths, breadths and heights of British Commercial Vehicles. It is to conform with these apparently arbitrary regulations that many home-market designs have developed a certain kinship with one another which would otherwise be difficult to explain. Those firms which have developed their export trade to the extent of designing special models have shown what can be done when they are " taken off the lead."

It should be noted that this book only attempts to cover vehicles in the 4-wheel class and upwards (with the exception of the Scammell ' Scarab ', which is in the full-size tractor class in all but wheel-arrangement) and only those powered by petrol or oil engines. To have included electrics and steam wagons, interesting though they may be, would have turned drastic compression into chronic congestion!

I should like to take this chance of thanking all the good friends in the Commercial Motor Industry whose ready co-operation with information and photographs helped to make this book possible.

D.J.W.

First published 1953
Reprinted 2001

ISBN 0 7110 2865 6

All rights reserved. No part of this book may be
reproduced or transmitted in any form or by any means,
electronic or mechanical, including photocopying, recording or by any information
storage and retrieval system, without permission from the Publisher in writing.

© Ian Allan Publishing Ltd 1953 / 2001

Published by Ian Allan Publishing

an imprint of Ian Allan Publishing Ltd, Hersham, Surrey, KT12 4RG.

Printed by Ian Allan Printing Ltd, Hersham, Surrey, KT12 4RG.

Code: 0110/A2

This is a facsimilie reprint of an original edition first published in 1953, and as
such, all advertisements are no longer valid.

A.E.C. — CROSSLEY — MAUDSLAY

Products of these three associated companies have now been standardized on the A.E.C. range. Vehicles produced in the Crossley and Maudslay factories still bear their distinctive badge on radiator and hub-caps, but chassis designation and layout are that of the corresponding A.E.C.

A.C.V. Sales, Ltd., Southall.
Range: *Goods vehicles for loads 7-15 tons, and maximum-dimension double- and single-deck passenger chassis.*
Goods: 7-8 ton 4-wheelers: *Monarch Mark III* (*Model 3451*)*:* Engine: A.E.C. 6-cylinder 7.7 litre diesel, 95 b.h.p. at 1,800 r.p.m. Alternative wheelbases: haulage 14′ 7″ and 16′ 7″, tipper 12′ 1″.
Mandator Mark III (*Model 3472*)*:* Engine: A.E.C. 6-cylinder 9.6 litre diesel, 120/125 b.h.p. at 1,800 r.p.m. Wheelbases as Monarch, but body space is somewhat reduced owing to larger engine being fitted. There is also a tractor for articulated trailer on the 12′ 1″ wheelbase. Mandator has 5-speed gearbox, Monarch 4-speed. 150/3 b.h.p. 11.3 litre engine can be fitted to Mandator if required.
12-ton 6-wheelers and 15-ton 8-wheelers: (*Mammoth Major Mark III*) (*Models 3671 and 3871 respectively*)*:* Engines and gearboxes as Mandator. 6-wheelers available with wheelbases 11′ 8½″ (tipper), 14′ 6½″, 16′ 9½″, and 18′ 9½″ (haulage); 8-wheelers have 14′ 6½″ and 18′ 9½″ only. Nominal width for all home models is 7′ 6″, for export models 8′ 0″.

Top: A.E.C. Regent Mk. III, fitted with Weymann highbridge body. *Centre:* A.E.C. Regal Mk. IV with Plaxton 'Venturer' body. *Bottom:* Maudslay 'Mammoth Major', showing A.E.C.-type radiator with Maudslay badge. *Heading:* A.E.C. Mandator Mk. III short-wheelbase tractor, with well-type semi-trailer.

5

Passenger: All models fitted as standard with 9.6-litre engine, (horizontal version for Regal Mark IV), and transmission is by fluid flywheel and 4-speed pre-selective epicyclic gearbox. 7.7 litre engine and synchromesh or constant-mesh gearboxes can be fitted to special order. Compressed-air operated gear-change and foot-brakes.

Regent Mark III: (Model 9613)*:* 16′ 4″ wheelbase double-decker; body width 7′ 6″ or 8′ 0″.

Regal Mark III: (Model 9621)*:* single-deck version (forward control), wheelbase 17′ 6″ (Home market), 19′ 3″ (Export).

Regal Mark IV: (Model 9822)*:* Underfloor-engine single-decker. Wheelbase 16′ 4″. Supplied as complete chassis for conventional body, or with outriggers for integral body construction.

ALBION

Albion Motors Ltd., Glasgow.
Range: Goods vehicles for loads from 3 to 14 tons and single-deck passenger vehicles of medium capacity.

Goods: 3-ton *Model FT*.21 **and 4-ton** *Model FT*.23*:* Engine: Albion EN 272 4-cylinder petrol, 53 b.h.p. at 2,800 r.p.m., with 4-speed gearbox. Wheelbases: Standard, 11′ 9″ (body lengths 13′ 3″ haulage and 13′ 6″ van), and Short, 9′ 6″ (10′ 9″ haulage and 11′ 0″ van body lengths). The FT.23 has larger tyres than the FT.21.

5-6 ton Models FT.3A and FT.37A ' Chieftan': Engines: FT.3A: EN 277 6-cylinder petrol, 80 b.h.p. at 2,800 r.p.m. FT.37A: Albion EN 286 4-cylinder diesel, 75 b.h.p. at 2,000 r.p.m. The latter has 5-speed gearbox. Alternative wheel-bases: 9′ 9″ for 4 cu. yard tipper body, 12′ 0″ and 14′ 0″ haulage, (body lengths 13′ 3″ and 15′ 3″ respectively) and 17′ 6″ for pantechnicon (up to 22′ long). 5 cu. yard tipper

Top: 'Victor' FT.39 passenger chassis with Harrington coach body.

Centre: HD. 57 short wheelbase 8-wheeler, with tipper body.

Bottom: 'Chieftan' FT.37A with extra-long wheelbase and special pantechnicon body.

Heading: FT.3AN 5-tonner working as cesspit emptier.

body can also be fitted to 12′ 0″ wheelbase. Wheelbases for the FT.37A are ½″ shorter, and bodies 9″ longer throughout, due to the greater compactness of the diesel engine. Van bodies for all haulage wheelbases are 3″ longer.

7½ *ton Model FT*.101*A ' Clydesdale ':* Engine (EN 286), wheelbases and body lengths as FT. 37A, but no van bodies supplied. A tractor for articulated trailer use is built on the 9′ 8½″ wheelbase, and there is also a 14′ 9″ base for 18′ 0″ platform. 12-ply tyres allow heavier loads to be carried.

Heavy Duty Range. *6-7 ton Model HD*.53: Engine: EN 253 6-cylinder diesel, 120 b.h.p. at 1,700 r.p.m., 5-speed gearbox. Alternative wheelbases: 9′ 3″ tractor, 11′ 3″ tipper, 16′ 0″ (20′ 0″ platform) and 13′ 9″ (17′ 3″ platform) haulage.

12-*ton Model HD*.55 single-steering 6-wheeler: EN 253 engine, and 5-speed gearbox. Alternative wheelbases: 13′ 6″ tipper, 16′ 0″ and 18′ 3″ haulage (body lengths 21′ 3″ and 24′ 3″ respectively).

15-*ton Model HD*.57 8-wheeler: Engine and gearbox as previous models; wheelbases 14′ 9″ tipper, or 18′ 3″ haulage (24′ 3″ platform). Van bodies, 3″ longer, can be supplied on all haulage chassis.

Passenger: *Model FT*.39*A Victor:* Engine: EN 286 4-cylinder diesel. Forward control, 5-speed gearbox. Wheelbase 16′ 0″ for bodies up to 26′ 3″ long, luxury coach seating up to 33 passengers. Width 7′ 6″. The ' Victor ' is the only conventional-engined chassis to employ a straight frame.

ATKINSON

Atkinson Lorries (1933) Ltd. Preston.
Range: *Goods vehicles for loads from 6-15 tons, and an underfloor-engine passenger chassis, all powered by Gardner diesel engines.*

8

Top: S1586 short-wheelbase tipper. *Bottom:* PM745H 'Alpha' lightweight under-floor-engine bus with Willowbrook body. *Heading:* L744 7½ tonner.

Goods: *6-ton Models:* (644 *Series.*) L644 and S644: Engine: 4LK 4-cylinder, 57 b.h.p. at 2,100 r.p.m. L644 is platform lorry, and S644 is tipper. L644LW is similar to L644, but has more powerful 4LW engine. Wheelbases: L644, 12′ 8″ for 16′ 0″ body; S644, 9′ 2″ for 5 cu. yards body.

7½-8-ton Models: (744, 745, & 746 *series*): Engines: 744: 4LW 4-cylinder, 75 b.h.p. at 1,700 r.p.m. 745: 5LW 5-cylinder, 94 b.h.p. at 1,700 r.p.m. 746: 6LW 6-cylinder, 112 b.h.p. at 1,700 r.p.m. Wheelbases: L744-6 (haulage) 13′ 6″ for 17′ 6″ body; L745L and L746L only: (long-wheelbase haulage): 15′ 0″ for 20′ 0″ body. S744-6 (tipper) 10′ 9″ for 6 cu. yards body; T744-6 (tractor for articulated trailer) 8′ 9″.

12-ton Models: (1266 *and* 1268 *series*.) Engines: 1266: 6LW; 1268: 8LW 8-cylinder, 150 b.h.p. at 1,700 r.p.m. (principally for export). 6-wheelers, with 2-wheel steering and 2-axle drive. M1266T has single-axle drive and trailing axle where required. Wheelbases: M1266 (haulage) 15′ 1½″ for 21′ 0″ body; S1266 (tipper) 13′ 3″ for 11 cu. yards body.

14-15 ton Models: (1586 *series*.) Engine: 6LW. Wheelbases: L1586 and L1586T (with trailing axle): 17′ 8¼″ for 24′ 0″ body (haulage); S1586: (tipper) 15′ 1½″ for 12 cu. yards body.

Passenger: (*PM* 744*H*, 745*H* & 746*H*) Engines: 4HLW, 5HLW and 6HLW respectively, these being the horizontal versions of the 4, 5, and 6 LW, for underfloor mounting. The PM744 and PM745 are new models for 1953 embodying lightweight alloy construction for economical service bus operation with 30′×8′ 44-seat bodies. Single rear-wheels are employed. The PM746, with more powerful engine and double rear-wheels is intended for luxury-coach bodywork. All wheelbases are 16′ 6″.

AUSTIN

Top: A70 Pick-up.　　*Centre:* 25 cwt 3-way Van.　　*Bottom:* 5-ton 'Loadstar' dropside lorry.　　*Heading:* A40 Van.

11

The Austin Motor Co. Ltd., Longbridge, Birmingham.

Range: Goods: Vans and lorries for loads up to 5 tons; passenger: hire car, ambulance and 26-seat coach chassis.

Light vans, pick-up and Ambulance: the A40 van and pick-up are based on the well-known " Devon " saloon and use the same engine; the A70 pick-up is based on the " Hereford " saloon, with the A70 engine. The latter is available with an alternative all-steel body by Anthony Hoists. The A125 Ambulance is built on the " Sheerline " car chassis, and uses the same 4-litre engine. More details of each of the chassis are given in the " ABC of British Cars."

Hire Car: Engine: A70, wheelbase 9′ 2⅝″. " Square " appearance, separate wings and headlamps; extensively used as London taxi in " half-cab " version.

25 cwt. Van: Engine: 4-cylinder 65-b.h.p. mounted between driver and passenger. 3-way loading by doors at rear and both sides. Capacity: 300 cubic yards. Broad radiator grille with chrome strips, similar to coach chassis.

2 and 5 ton lorries: Engine: 6-cylinder 100 b.h.p. Wheelbases: 2-ton haulage: 11′ 2″ for 11′ 6″ body; 5-ton haulage: 13′ 1¾″ for 14′ 0″ body; 5-ton tipper: 9′ 7″. Normal control, radiators have chrome-strip grilles. Headlamps, but not side-lamps, built into wings. The Austin Fire-engine, equipped by John Kerr of Manchester, and the 4-wheel drive 1-ton military vehicle are based on these chassis. Another newly-developed military vehicle is the " Champ ", similar in purpose to the American " Jeep ".

Bus and Coach Chassis: Engine: 4-litre 100 b.h.p. Wheelbase: 15′ 0″. Used mainly as 26-30 seat private hire coach with bodywork by various builders. A standard service bus with Mulliner body is marketed for export with seats for from 30 to 42 passengers. Perkins P6 diesel engine can be fitted if required.

Bedford 10-12 Van. In background, a 4-ton tipper of the former design.

BEDFORD

Vauxhall Motors Ltd., Luton.

Range: *Goods: vans 10 and 25 cwt., lorries 1-10 tons. Passenger: medium-capacity bus and coach chassis.*

Goods: 10-12 cwt. Van: Engine 4-cylinder petrol, 40 b.h.p. at 4,000 r.p.m., as used in "Wyvern" car. 135 cu. feet body, side doors of which slide back outside body. At front, a wide, low grille with two bold chrome strips. 5-seat Utility, small ambulance, and pick-up with extended cab canopy to protect passengers also provided on the same chassis.

20-25 cwt. Models: Engine: 6-cylinder petrol, 76 b.h.p. at 3.200 r.p.m. Wheelbase: 9' 11", with single rear wheels. 300 cubic feet capacity all-metal van body by Spurling has rear or 3-way loading, and the standard all-steel pick-up body is 8' 3" long. Special bodies include ambulances by several builders, and an "airport" type light bus by Spurlings.

3-ton Models: Engine: 76 b.h.p. as above. Short wheelbase: 9' 11" for 2¾ cu. yards tipper body or use with special bodies, e.g., road-sweepers. Long wheelbase: 11' 11" for 11' 7" dropside body. Double rear-wheels fitted, and if larger tyres and helper springs are used, greater loads can be carried.

4- and 5-ton Models: Engine: 6-cylinder petrol, 84 b.h.p. at 3,100 r.p.m., or Perkins P6 6-cylinder diesel, 83 b.h.p. at 2,400 r.p.m. Short wheelbase: 10' 0" for 4.4 cu. yards tipper body, or as tractor with Scammell trailer and automatic coupling, for loads up to 8 tons. Long wheelbase: 13' 11" for 14' 0½" dropside body. 4- and 5-ton models have identical dimensions, but the latter use larger tyres and extra springing.

7-ton Models (The " Big Bedfords "): Engine: 6-cylinder petrol, 110 b.h.p. at 3,200 r.p.m. Short-wheelbase: 9' 8" for U-section all-steel tipper body of 6 cu. yards capacity. Long-wheelbase: 13' 0" for 16' 0" dropside body. Extra-short wheelbase: 7' 2", a tractor for articulated use with Scammell trailer, for loads up to 10 tons.

The " Middleweight " models (1-5 tons) are all fitted with the re-designed all-steel cab and have normal control. Bonnet is of simple design, with separate built-in head and side-lights and grille composed of three horizontal bars bearing chrome strips. The 7-10 ton " Big Bedfords " have forward-control all-steel cab, the grille has seven horizontal chromed bars.

Bedfords, the most-used commercial vehicles in Britain, can be seen with a large variety of special bodies in addition to the standard ones mentioned above. These include fire-engines, pantechnicons, tankers, mobile shops and every type of body for municipal sanitary purposes.

Top: New 'Middleweight' 4–5 ton long wheelbase truck.

Centre: "Big Bedford" 7-ton tipper with U-section steel body.

Bottom: Duple 'Vega' coach body on "Big Bedford" passenger chassis.

Passenger: Engine: 110 b.h.p. as above. Wheelbase: 17′ 2″, for body length of 28′ 11¾″. Body width can be 8′ 0″ or 7′ 6″. Standard coach body is Duple Vega 35-37 seater, but chassis can be supplied for other builders. Frontal finish is similar to other " Big Bedfords ".

14

BRADFORD

The Bradford 10 cwt. Van

Jowett Cars, Ltd., Idle, Bradford.
Range: *10 cwt. van and dropside lorry.*

The same chassis and engine is used for all Bradford vehicles, the engine being of the traditional 2-cylinder horizontally-opposed type, giving 25 b.h.p. at 3,500 r.p.m., transmitted through a 3-speed gearbox. **The Van** body has a capacity of 93 cubic feet, and the **dropside lorry** a platform 5′ 6″ long. Utility bodies are also provided, and in each case a bonnet of the conventional type is fronted by divided radiator grille, composed of horizontal and vertical wire slats. One-piece head and parking lamps are mounted externally on the wings.

BRISTOL

Bristol Tramways and Carriage Co. Ltd., Bristol.
Note: This company, which is not connected with the Bristol Aeroplane Company (the company which makes Bristol cars), began manufacturing bus chassis for its own services, developed by supplying them to other operators, and has now been taken over by the British Transport Commission as one of the assets of the "Tilling" Group, to which it belonged. Since nationali-

Eastern Coachworks 41-seat coach body on Bristol LS underfloor-engine chassis

zation, Bristol have supplied bus chassis only to B.T.C. companies, mainly with bodies by Eastern Coachworks, a former Eastern Counties subsidiary also taken over by the B.T.C. To meet the Commission's requirements, an 8-wheeled 15-ton goods vehicle has recently been produced by Bristol, the first example of a series of standard types for service with the Road Haulage Executive (British Road Services).

Apart from this goods vehicle, the **Bristol range** *includes double and single-deck maximum capacity vehicles of forward control layout, and a single-deck underfloor-engine unit for integral-construction bodywork.*

Goods Vehicle: 15-ton model: *(HG6L type):* Engine: Leyland 600/2 9.8 litre diesel, 125 b.h.p. at 1,800 r.p.m., transmitted through single dry-plate clutch and 5-speed gearbox of Bristol make. This vehicle is 7′ 6″ wide, and has the maximum legal overall length of 30′. Recognition features include large double windscreen, built-in head and side lamps, heavy front bumper with number-plate in centre, and vertical-bar radiator grille adapted from the well-known Bristol shape.

Passenger Vehicles: *K-type* forward control double-decker, and *L-type* forward-control single-decker: Standard engine: Gardner 5LW 5-cylinder oil engine, of 85 b.h.p. at 1,700 r.p.m., with the alternative of the Gardner 6LW 6-cylinder 112 b.h.p. engine. Bristol-made clutch and gearbox. Main difference between the two types is that the 'L' has a longer wheelbase and a 5-speed gearbox incorporating an 'overtop' for faster and more economical long-distance running.

LS-type: 'underframe' for Eastern Coachworks coach or service bus body. Alternative engines (underfloor): Bristol 8-litre or Gardner 6LW or 5LW. 5-speed gearbox has synchronmesh on 2nd, 3rd and 4th speeds. Construction incorporates aluminium alloys for greatest lightness.

16

Top: K6B chassis with Eastern Coachworks highbridge body.   *Bottom:* HG6L 15-tonner produced to B.R.S. specification.

The Bristol Company has also produced two experimental 'Lodekka'' buses, a design which seeks to overcome the disadvantages of the normal type of 'lowbridge' bus of the side-gangway type by lowering the level of both decks. This is achieved by dividing the transmission and reducing ground clearance.

COMMER

Commer Cars, Ltd., Luton.
Range: *Goods vehicles for loads from* 10 *cwt. to* 12 *tons, and a medium-capacity passenger chassis.*
Goods: Express Delivery Van: Engine: 37.5 b.h.p. at 4,200 r.p.m. petrol, 4-speed synchromesh gearbox with steering-column control. Engine and transmission are as Hillman Minx car, which the van resembles in frontal and dashboard appearance. Body space: 100 cubic feet, for loads up to 10 cwt.
25 cwt. vans: Engine: 50 b.h.p. 4-cylinder petrol, 4-speed gearbox. Available with forward or normal control. Forward-control model has 309 cubic feet body with two sliding side-doors in addition to rear doors. Radiator grille with horizontal slats surrounded by chrome band projects a few inches forward. Normal control model has outward-opening doors and body capacity of nearly 200 cubic feet. There is also a 25-cwt. dropside truck mounted on the 10′ 0″ forward-control wheelbase, with body length of 9′ 9″.
Note: Normal-control Commers are distinguished by a horizontal bar chrome radiator grille commencing well below moulded bonnet-brow, with head and side lamps built into wings. They are styled ' superpoise ', and incorporate a patented method of mounting cab, bonnet, wings and bumper as a unit direct onto the chassis.
2-3 tonners: Engine: 6-cylinder petrol, developing 85 b.h.p. at 3,100 r.p.m., 4-speed gearbox. Alternative wheelbases: standard, 12′ 11″ for 12′ 0″ dropside body, and tipper, 10′ 2″.
3-4 tonners: Engine and wheelbase as 2-3 tonners, but larger tyres are used, dropside body is 2′ longer and Perkins P6V diesel engine can be fitted to these, and to larger forward-control models. This unit develops 79 b.h.p. at 2,400 r.p.m.
5- tonners (Normal Control): Engine: As 3-4 tonners. Alternative wheelbases: haulage, 13′ 11″, for 15′ 6″ body; tipper,

Top: 25 cwt. normal control 'superpoise' van.   *Centre:* 7-ton tipper with underfloor engine.   *Bottom:* 'Avenger' passenger chassis with Plaxton coach body.   *Heading:* 3–4 ton 'superpoise' long-wheelbase dropsider.

19

11′ 8″, and tractor 10′ 2″, intended for use with Hands automatic-coupling trailer for loads in the 8-10 ton class.

5-7 tonners (Forward Control): Engine: 6-cylinder petrol, 109 b.h.p. at 3,000 r.p.m., mounted underfloor slightly off horizontal. Wheelbases: 5- and 7-ton haulage, 11′ 9″ for 15′ 6″ body, the 7-tonners having heavier-duty tyres and springs; 7-ton long-wheelbase: 13′ 6″ for 18′ 0″ body; 6½-7 ton tippers, 9′ 7″, and tractor, 7′ 9″. Tractors are for use with Hands articulated trailer to carry 10 and 12-ton loads, the latter having lower-ratio gearbox. These models have radiator concealed by a number of horizontal bars, surmounted by four wider decorative bars incorporating the filler cap. The Eaton electrically-controlled 2-speed rear axle can be fitted on all models over 5 tons, to give an extra range of gears.

Passenger: "*Avenger*". Engine: 6- cylinder 109 b.h.p. petrol, with a 4-speed gearbox and 2 speed rear-axle if required. Wheelbase: 15′ 9″ for bodies up to 27′ 6″ in length and 7′ 6″ or 8′ 0″ wide, seating up to 33 as luxury coach or 35 as service bus. Bodies by Plaxtons, Churchills and Harringtons are recommended, but classis supplied for coachwork by other builders if required.

DAIMLER

Transport Vehicles (Daimler) Ltd., Coventry.

Range: *Passenger vehicles only, maximum capacity double- and single-deck forward control chassis, and an underfloor-engine single-decker; also an ambulance. All vehicles fitted with fluid flywheel and pre-selective gearbox.*

CD 650: Engine: Daimler CD 650 vertical 6-cylinder 10.6 litre diesel, giving 125 b.h.p. if governed at 1,800 r.p.m., or 134 b.h.p. at 2,000 r.p.m. As double decker, wheelbase is 16′ 4″, width 7′ 6″ or 8′ 0″. As single-decker, wheelbase of 20′ 0″ is provided for bodies 8′ 0″ wide and length in excess of

Top: Daimler CVD 6 with Metropolitan-Cammell highbridge body. *Centre:* A CD650 for the home market — in the service of a Co. Durham operator. *Bottom:* The Daimler Ambulance. *Heading:* The 'Freeline' chassis with all working parts below frame level.

British legal maximum, for high seating-capacity service overseas. Double-decker has 4-speed gearbox. single-decker, 5-speed. These are compressed air-operated, and power-assisted steering can be fitted if required. CD 650 is principally an export chassis, and is distinguished by its wide radiator with vertical bars and fluted top.

CVD 6, CVG 5 and CVG 6: Engines: Daimler 6-cylinder 8.6 litre (109 b.h.p. at 1,800 r.p.m.), Gardner 5-cylinder 7-litre (94 b.h.p. at 1,700 r.p.m.), and Gardner 6-cylinder 8.4 litre (112 b.h.p. at 1,700 r.p.m.) respectively. Double-deck wheelbase: 16′ 3$\frac{5}{32}$″; single-deck: 17′ 2½″ or 19′ 0″, frames for either 7′ 6″ or 8′ 0″ bodies being available. Gearboxes are four-speed pre-selector, mechanically operated. These are the standard chassis for the home market, as supplied to many municipal operators.

CLG and CLD double-deck chassis: Engine: Gardner 5LW (standard) with Gardner 6LW or Daimler CVD 6 as alternatives. Wheelbase, 16′ 4″, widths 7′ 6″ or 8′ 0″ as required. Special lightweight construction; if used with lightweight body, unladen weight is up to one ton lighter than normal double-deck vehicles.

" *Freeline* ": Engine: D650H 10.6 litre (Horizontal version of CD 650); alternative: Gardner 6HLW 8.4 litre (horizontal). Alternative wheelbases: 17′ 6″ (7′ 6″ or 8′ 0″ wide) or 16′ 4″ (8′ 0″ wide only). Compressed air operates 5-speed pre-selective gearbox, brakes and, if required, body doors and power-assisted steering. Chassis is designed to eliminate all obstructions to bodybuilding above frame level.

Ambulance: Engine: 4-litre petrol, 110 b.h.p. at 3,600 r.p.m. This chassis, specially designed for the purpose, incorporates independent front-wheel suspension. Special body is by Barkers.

DENNIS

Dennis Bros. Ltd., Guildford.
Range: *Goods vehicles for loads from 5-12 tons, and single- and double-deck passenger vehicles.*
Goods: *Pax 5-6 tonners:* Alternative Engines: Dennis petrol 70 b.h.p. side-valve, or 80 b.h.p. overhead valve (1,800 r.p.m.); Perkins P6 diesel (70 b.h.p. at 2,200 r.p.m.). Alternative wheelbases available: 9′ 6″, 11′ 6″, 12′ 10″, normal or forward control. Also a normal control rigid tractor, 8 3$\frac{3}{8}$″ wheelbase.

Opposite: *Top:* 'Horla' tractor with semi-trailer. *Centre:* 'Centaur' 6-7 tonner used as a tanker. *Bottom:* 'Lance' single-decker.

'Jubilant' 12-ton platform lorry

Horla tractor is similar and uses any of above engines, but is fitted with Scammell automatic coupling gear. Tractors with trailers can take loads up to 8 tons. *Pax* platform lengths: Normal control: 10' 11"-15' 11"; forward control: 14' 2½"-18' 5½". Tipper body capacities: 3½-5 cu. yards.

Centaur 6-7 tonner (forward control). Engine: Dennis 6-cylinder diesel, 75 b.h.p. at 2,000 r.p.m. Wheelbases, 13' 6" (18' 3½" platform) or 10' 6" (6 cu. yards tipper).

Max and Max 6, 6-7 tonners: Engine (Max): Dennis 0.4 4-cylinder diesel (80 b.h.p. at 1,800 r.p.m.); (Max 6): Dennis 0.6 6-cylinder diesel (100 b.h.p. at 1,800 r.p.m.) Wheelbases: Max: 14' 0" (18' 11" platform) or 12' 0" (tipper). Max 6: 15' 6" (21' 1" platform), 10' 11" (tipper) or 9' 6" (tractor).

Jubilant 12-ton 6-wheeler: Engine: Dennis 0.6. Wheelbases: 17' 10½" (24' 6" platform) or 13' 6" (tipper).

Passenger: *Single-deck Falcon:* Engine: Dennis 75-b.h.p. diesel, as in Centaur lorry. Wheelbase 17' 1" for 30-33 seat body.

Lancet: Engine: Dennis 0.6 100 b.h.p. 6-cylinder diesel. Wheelbases: 17' 5" for 27' 6"×7' 6" body, or 18' 6" for 30' 0"×8' 0" body.

Double-deck: *Lance:* Engine: Dennis 0.6, wheelbase, 16' 3".

DODGE

Dodge Bros. (Britain) Ltd., Kew.

Range: *Goods vehicles for loads from 2 to 6 tons.*

2-3 tonners: *Model 64:* Engine: Dodge 6-cylinder petrol, 109 b.h.p. at 3,600 r.p.m. Wheelbase; 11' 9" for 11' 6" dropside body, or 12' 3" van body, with capacity of 450 cu. feet.

Top: Model 64 2–3 ton van. *Bottom:* Model 123 6–ton tipper. The 5–ton long wheelbase Model 105P6 is illustrated on the title page.

5 tonners: *Model* 105: Engine: As Model 64. Wheelbase: 13′ 9″, for 15′ 0″ dropside body. *Model* 103/P6 has Perkins P6 diesel engine, giving 83 b.h.p. at 2,400 r.p.m. 9′ 1″ wheelbase used for 5 cu. yards tipper body. *Model* 105/P6 has similar frame to Model 105, but uses P6 engine.

6 tonners: *Model* 123: Engine: Dodge petrol, 114 b.h.p. at 3.600 r.p.m., with 9′ 11″ wheelbase for tipper (as 103/P6). *Model* 125 also uses the 114 b.h.p. engine, wheelbase and body being as Model 105. 6-tonners are fitted with larger (12-ply) tyres.

All Dodge chassis are available for special bodybuilding, and the short-wheelbase chassis can be adapted for use as a tractor with articulated trailer.

E.R.F.

E.R.F. Ltd., Sandbach.
Range: *Goods vehicles for loads from 6 to 15 tons, all powered by Gardner oil engines.*
4-wheeled models:
LK.4.4. (6 tonner). Engine: 4LK, 57 b.h.p. at 2,100 r.p.m. Radiator projects forward. Wheelbases: Standard, 12′ 8″ for 16′ 0″ body, Medium 11′ 2″ for 14′ 0″ body, and tipper, 8′ 8″ (10′ 0″ body).
4.4, 5.4, *and* 6.4 (7-8 *tonners*). Engines, 4LW (75 b.h.p.), 5LW (94 b.h.p.), and 6LW (112 b.h.p.) respectively. Standard wheelbases: 14′ 0″ for 18′ 0″ body; medium wheelbases: 12′ 6⅞ for 16′ 0″ body. Tippers have 12′ 6″ bodies, and wheelbases from 11′ 1″ to 11′ 3″, according to engine used, and tractors for use with articulated trailers and loads of 10-15 tons, 8′ 7″ wheelbase; (8′ 5″ only with 5LW engine). *Model 4.4G* is almost identical with 4.4., but the usual wide radiator grille traversed by the E.R.F. insignia is replaced by a smaller gauze-covered elipse surrounded by heavy chromed band. Side lights are built into the wings.
6-wheeled models:
5.6 *TS* (9-10 *tonner*): Engine: 5LW. Twin-steering model, with 17′ 2″ wheelbase for 20′ 0″ body.
5.6 *and* 6.6 (12½ *tonners*): Engines: 5LW and 6LW respectively. Wheelbases: Standard, 16′ 6″ for 22′ 0″ body; tipper, 12′ 9″ for 16′ 0″ body.
8-wheeled models:
6.8 (15 *tonner*): Engine: 6LW, driving on both rear axles. Wheelbases: Standard, 18′ 0″ for 24′ 0″ body; Medium, 16′ 6″ for 22′ 0″ body, and tipper, 14′ 6″ for 18′ 0″ body.

Top: LK 4·4 fitted with van body. Centre: 4·4G showing modernized radiator.
Bottom: 6·8 15–tonner with dropside body. Heading: 5·6TS 9–10 tonner with
platform body.

FODEN

Fodens Ltd., Sandbach.
Range: *Goods vehicles for loads from 6-15 tons under home
conditions, and various special chassis primarily for service under
arduous conditions overseas. Also a rear-engined passenger
chassis.*
Goods: 4-wheelers:
6-tonner: Model OG 4/6. Engine: Gardner 4LK, 57 b.h.p. at
2,100 r.p.m. with 5-speed gearbox. Alternative wheelbases:
12′ 7¼″ for standard 16′ 0″ body, and 8′ 0″ for tipper or articulated tractor.
7½ tonners: Models FG 4/7½, FG 5/7½ and FG 6/7½. Engines:
Gardner 4LW, 5LW and 6LW respectively, (see corresponding
E.R.F. models). Alternative wheelbases: Standard 13′ 9″
for body 17′ 0″-18′ 0″ long, according to engine used; 10′ 3¾″
for tipper, and 7′ 10½″ for tractor intended for articulated use.
6-wheelers: *12-ton Models FG 5/12 and FG 6/12:* Engines
5LW and 6LW respectively. Wheelbases: Standard, 17′ 6″
for 24′ 0″ body, and tipper 11′ 0″.
8- wheelers: *15-ton Model FG 6/15:* Engine: 6LW. Wheelbases: standard, 13′ 7½″ for 24′ 6″ body, and tipper, 9′ 9″.

All models using the 6LW engine can be fitted alternatively
with the Foden FD 6 two-stroke diesel unit, developing 126
b.h.p. at 2,000 r.p.m.
Special Heavy Goods Vehicles: Fodens produce a number of
special tractors, with 4-, 6-, and 8-wheel arrangements, for
articulated or independent use in special haulage or forestry
work. There is also a " dumper ", with massively-protected
tipping body for quarry use. 6- and 8-wheeled heavy export

Top: OG 4/6 with platform body.

Centre: The Foden 'Dumper' showing the protective cab-shield.

Bottom: This view of the rear-engined passenger chassis shows the accessibility of the power unit.

Heading: FG 5/12 with platform body.

models use the Gardner 8LW 150 b.h.p. engine. All models are available with 8- or 12-speed gearboxes. In the latter case, a fairly low 4-speed box is supplemented by an underdrive for really arduous conditions, and an overdrive for normal road use.

Passenger: *Model PVRF* 6; Engine: Foden FD 6 two-stroke diesel (126 b.h.p. at 2,000 r.p.m., with 112 b.h.p. Gardner 6LW as alternative. Engine is mounted vertically and at right-angles to main frame at rear of chassis, with radiator and fuel tank behind the rear wheels on the offside. This is the only rear-engined British chassis, though the layout, for which decreased internal noise and increased accessibility are claimed, is widely used in America and on the Continent. Wheelbase is 16′ 6″ and frame 29′ 5″ long, for 30′ 0″ by 8′ 0″ maximum-dimension body. Chassis is widely used by continental tour operators and luxury bodies by James Whitson, Gurney Nutting, Bellhouse Hartwell and Plaxtons are recommended, each designed for 41 seats. A 43-seat service bus version by Lawton with front entrance can also be fitted.

FORD THAMES

The Ford Motor Company Ltd., Dagenham.

Range: *Goods vehicles for loads from 5 cwt. to 8 tons.*

5 *cwt. Van*: Engine: Ford 4-cylinder side-valve petrol, 23.4 b.h.p. at 4,000 r.p.m., as used in Anglia car, from which this model is developed. Body capacity is 65 cu. feet.

10 *cwt. Van*: Engine: Ford 4-cylinder petrol, 30.1 b.h.p. at 4,000 r.p.m., as used in Prefect car. Body space, 120 cu. feet.

Top: 10 cwt. model with all-steel pick-up body. *Centre:* 5 cwt. van.
Bottom: 4 cu. yard tipper on extra-short 4-5 ton wheelbase. *Heading:* The
Thames 2-ton truck.

31

Semi-forward control, with short, wide bonnet, fronted by grille with horizontal bars divided by a vertical bar. One-piece lights mounted on wings, as on 5 cwt. There is also a steel-bodied pick-up version, with 28.3 cu. feet body capacity.

2-8 ton models: All Thames vehicles of 2 tons capacity upwards are powered by the well-known V8 petrol engine, which incorporates two banks of four cylinders mounted at 90 degrees to one another and 45 degrees to the vertical. This develops 85 b.h.p. at 3,500 r.p.m. and is transmitted through 4-speed gearbox. Alternative engine on models from 3 tons upwards: Perkins P6 diesel, 73 b.h.p. at 2,400 r.p.m. These models have " alligator " bonnets with grille of seven horizontal bars, and separate head- and side-lights built into the wings.

2-*ton Van*: Capacity, 450 cu. feet. Sliding doors on both sides.

2- and 3-*ton Trucks* : Wheelbase: 10′ 8″ for 11′ 0″ dropside body. 3-tonner has 8-ply instead of 6-ply tyres.

4-5 *tonners*: Short wheelbase models as 2-3 tonners, with 10-ply tyres. Long wheelbase: 13′ 1″ for 14′ 6″ dropside body. Extra-short wheelbase of 10′ 2″ provided for tipper bodies of 4 cu. yards capacity.

8-*ton Models*: The same 10′ 2″ chassis is also produced as articulated-trailer tractor, for loads up to 8 tons. There is also a 6-wheeler range, called the " Sussex ", with 10′ 8″ or 13′ 1″ wheelbases, intended for work under very arduous conditions. " Sussex " is only standard production 6-wheeler fitted with petrol engine.

Standard bodies for municipal cleansing services include a refuse collector and a gulley emptier, mounted on the 3-ton chassis. The " Jekta " body, designed by Walker (*q.v.*) and County Commercial Cars Ltd., as a more efficient means of ejecting a bulk load than the usual tipper, is mounted on the 5-ton chassis. In addition, a wide variety of bodies for special purposes is available for use on Thames chassis. Although no chassis specially designed for passenger use is built, the 5-ton long-wheelbase model is suitable, and extensively used for passenger bodies seating 30-33 persons.

GUY

Guy Motors Ltd., Wolverhampton.

Range: *Goods vehicles for 2-6 ton loads, and passenger chassis for single- and double-deck bodies, forward control and under-floor-engined types.*

Goods: *Wolf 2-3 tonner*: Alternative engines: Guy petrol, 50 b.h.p. at 2,400 r.p.m. or Perkins P4 diesel, 46 b.h.p. at 2,200 r.p.m. There are two wheelbases, 10′ 6″ and 13′ 0″, suitable

Top: Wolf 2-3 ton van with petrol engine. *Centre:* Otter 5-6 tonner with all-steel cab and diesel engine. *Bottom:* 'Vixen' passenger coach with petrol engine.

'Arab' underfloor-engine chassis with Willowbrook coachwork.

for dropside-lorry or van bodies. Wolf and Vixen models have the conventional Guy radiator, divided vertically and with wire-mesh covering.

Vixen 4-tonner: Engine: Guy petrol, 58 b.h.p. at 2,400 r.p.m. Alternative wheelbases, 10′ 6″, 13′ 0″ and 14′ 9″ for dropside and van bodies, the first being also suitable for tipper body.

Otter 5-6 tonner: Engine: Guy 58 b.h.p. petrol or Gardner 4LK or Perkins P6 diesels. Wheelbases are 13′ 0″ and 14′ 9″ for normal haulage as for the Vixen, and, in addition, a 9′ 9″ base for tipper and a 9′ 0″ one for tractor used with articulated trailer, are available. Modernised all-steel cab and undivided vertical-bar radiator are fitted.

Passenger: *Vixen and Otter Light Passenger Chassis:* Engines: Vixen, 58 b.h.p. petrol only; Otter, same petrol engine, or 4LK or P6 diesel. Chassis are similar in layout to corresponding goods models, with 14′ 9″ wheelbases, suitable for 29-33 seat bodies.

Arab Range: This now includes 3 models: forward-control double-deck, forward-control single-deck, and underfloor engine single-deck. All three can be fitted with Gardner 5LW or 6LW engine (5HLW or 6HLW horizontal versions in the underfloor-engine model). Transmission by 4-speed synchro-mesh gearbox or fluid flywheel and epicyclic box. Home-market wheelbases are 16′ 4″ for double-decker and underfloor-engine single-decker, and 18′ 5″ for forward-control single-decker. Body widths can be 7′ 6″ or 8′ 0″, and lengths up to the maximum legal 30′ 0″. Guy Motors supply most chassis for outside body-building, but also supply their own service bus bodies, mostly built to Park Royal design.

JENSEN

Jensen Motors, Ltd., West Bromwich.
Range: *JNSN 6-ton lightweight commercial vehicle, and Jen-tug 4-wheeled articulated tractor, and trailer.*
JNSN: Engine: Perkins P6, 83 b.h.p. at 2,400 r.p.m. Standard wheelbase, 16′ 2″ for 23′ 0″ body; short wheelbase, 12′ 8½″ for 18′ 0″ body. Constructed throughout of aluminium alloy,

being an underframe for integral construction with lightweight dropside, pantechnicon and other special bodies.

Jen-Tug: Engine: Austin A40, 40 b.h.p. at 4,300 r.p.m. A 4-wheeled "mechanical horse" for loads up to 3 tons. Semi-trailer automatically coupled by patent single-ramp system. Engine housed on frame behind cab. Standard platform trailer, 13′ 0″ long.

Top: The Jen-tug, with semi-trailer attached.
Left The 'JNSN' underframe, showing outriggers for integral body construction.

KARRIER

Karrier Motors, Ltd., Luton.
Range: *" Low-loading " goods chassis for loads from 2-5 tons, and a passenger chassis for 14-seat body. Karrier vehicles are designed principally for use with a variety of special bodies as municipal sanitary vehicles. The " Bantam " 2-tonner is also available with standard platform and dropside bodies, and the " Bantam " tractor is suitable for articulated trailer use for loads of 4-5 tons.*
" Bantam " 2-*tonner:* Engine: 4-cylinder petrol, 48 b.h.p. Wheelbase, 8′ 2″ for 11′ 4″ body. Tractor version has 6′ 3″ wheelbase. Two types of automatic coupling are available: ' BK ' for 4-point trailer support, and ' J ' for 3-point support. *" Gamecock "* 3-4 *tonner:* Engine: 6-cylinder petrol, 85 b.h.p. at 3,100 r.p.m. Alternative wheelbases, 9′ 7″ and 11′ 9″ for body lengths of 13′ 5$\frac{7}{16}$″ and 15′ 11$\frac{3}{4}$″ respectively.

All above vehicles have forward-control, and radiator frontage with 5 broad, equally-spaced apertures. The *Type* " RSC " Karrier-Yorkshire road-sweeper is a normal control vehicle, and has bonnet design similar to normal-control Commers, with left-hand drive and the 85 b.h.p. engine.
Passenger: The 14-seat Passenger Model has the " Bantam " 4-cylinder engine and 10′ 0″ wheelbase. Standard body is by Readings of Portsmouth.

Left: 'Gamecock' 3-4 tonner with 'Derby'-type refuse-collection body.

Right: The Reading-bodied 14-seat passenger model.

LEYLAND

Leyland Motors, Ltd., Leyland, Lancs.
Range: *Goods vehicles for loads from 7 to 14 tons, and passenger vehicles for double- and single-deck bodies.*
Goods: *Comet '90' 7½-ton range (Model ECO 2):* Engine: Leyland 6-cylinder diesel, 90 b.h.p. at 2,200 r.p.m.; 5-speed gearbox and Eaton 2-speed rear-axle. Alternative wheelbases:
ECO 2.1R: 14' 2" for 16' 6" platform body.
ECO 2.2R and ECO 2.3R: 10' 5" for tipper or tractor respectively.
ECO 2.4R: 15' 3" for 18' 0" platform body.
ECO 2.5R: 8' 7" tractor, for Scammell automatic-coupling trailer.
    Comet '90s' have semi-forward control, and distinctive bonnet has broad horizontal flutes divided by chrome strip, and deep recesses in the angles of the "alligator" bonnet-top.
Forward-control models: These include all remaining Leyland goods vehicles normally built for the home market. Engine: Leyland 6-cylinder diesel, 125 b.h.p. at 1,800 r.p.m. Standard cab of aluminium construction, with rectangular divided wire-mesh radiator frontage.
Beaver 7-ton 4-wheeler: Model 12.B1: 15' 0" wheelbase for 20' 0" platform body.
Model 12.B3: 12' 6" wheelbase for tipper body.
Model 12.B7: 8' 6" wheelbase for tractor.
Steer 9½-ton twin-steering 6-wheeler: Model 15.S1: 19' 0" wheelbase for 21' 6" platform body.

Hippo 12-*ton single-steering 6-wheeler:*
Model 19.H1: 15′ 6″ wheelbase for 21′ 6″ platform body.
Model 19.H3: 13′ 6″ wheelbase for tipper body.
Model 19.H7: 17′ 9″ wheelbase for 24′ 6″ platform body.
Octopus 14-*ton 8-wheeler:* Model 22.01: 17′ 9″ wheelbase for 24′ 6″ platform body. Model 22.03: 15′ 6″ wheelbase for tipper body.

Goods Vehicles for Export. All the above are available for export, although only the Comet and the Octopus are built with left-hand drive. In addition, a completely separate 4- and 6-wheeled range, called 'Super Beavers' and 'Super Hippos' respectively are built for export only. These have normal-control and conventional bonnets, with traditional Leyland grilles. All use the 125 b.h.p. engine, and are available with left- or right-hand drive in a wide range of wheelbases.

Passenger: *Titan double-deck chassis:* Models PD.2/12 and PD.2/20: Engine: Leyland 6-cylinder diesel, 125 b.h.p. at 1,800 r.p.m. Wheelbase: 16′ 5″ for 27′ 0″ body.

Tiger forward-control single-deck chassis: Models PS.2/12A and PS.2/13A: 125 b.h.p. engine and 18′ 9″ wheelbase for 30′ 0″ body.

Tiger Cub underfloor-engine single-deck chassis: Model PSUC/1/1: Engine: Leyland 6-cylinder diesel, 90 b.h.p. at 2,200 r.p.m., horizontal version, mounted amidships. Wheelbase: 16′ 2″ for 30′ 0″ bus body, seating up to 44 persons. Unladen weight of under 6 tons achieved by elimination of dead weight and wide use of light alloys.

Royal Tiger underfloor-engine single-deck chassis: Models PSU.1/13 (for bus body) and PSU.1/16 (for coach). Horizontal version of 125 b.h.p. engine; wheelbase 15′ 7″ for 30′ 0″ body. Standard fittings include a rear drop-frame extension on the PSU.1/13, and compressed air brakes on the PSU.1/16.

Top: Hippo Model 19H1 with platform body. *Centre:* 'Tiger Cub' lightweight bus with Saunders-Roe bodywork. *Bottom:* 'Titan' double-decker with Leyland all-metal body. *Opposite:* Comet '90' tanker.

Olympic integrally-constructed bus: Model HR.44/96, with 44-seat M.C.W. body built on Leyland running units. Engine and wheelbase as for Royal Tiger.

The Comet '90' chassis has been used for passenger purposes mainly overseas, although some of these normal-control vehicles have been acquired by British operators. With the exception of the Tiger Cub, all other Layland passenger chassis are available for export, the Royal Tiger and Olympic only being available with left-hand as well as right-hand drive. Extra-long wheelbases are provided where local conditions permit.

Leyland Motors have extensive bodyworks which can provide suitable passenger bodies for the chassis described above, but all complete chassis are available for bodying elsewhere if required.

MORRIS — MORRIS-COMMERCIAL

Morris Motors, Ltd., Cowley, Oxford.
Morris-Commercial Cars, Ltd., Birmingham.
Range: (*Morris Motors*): *5-cwt. van, and half-ton van and pick up.* (*Morris-Commercial*): *Goods vehicles for loads from 10 cwt. to 5 tons.*
Note: The commercial vehicles made by Morris Motors are directly based on Morris cars—the 5-cwt van on the range of " Eight " cars produced up to 1947, and the half-tonner on the present " Oxford " saloon.

Above : FV13/5 5-tonner with special body built in Malaya. *Opposite, top :* Morris 5cwt van. *Centre :* New LD.2. 1½-ton van shown at the Commercial Motor Show. *Bottom :* The normal-control 5-tonner (NVS 13/5) with 100 b.h.p. petrol engine.

5-cwt. Van: Engine: Morris 4-cylinder side-valve petrol, 27.5 b.h.p. at 4,400 r.p.m. Wheelbase 7' 5", body capacity 79 cu. feet. Normal control, rounded radiator grille with horizontal bars, One-piece head- and parking-lamps mounted on wings.

Half-ton (*formerly " Cowley "*) **Van and Pick-up:** Engine: Morris 4-cylinder petrol, 41 b.h.p. at 4,000 r.p.m. Engine and frontal design, including bonnet, heavy cross-barred grille, cab fittings and ' V ' windscreen, similar to ' Oxford ' car. Wheelbase: 8' 1"; van body capacity, 120 cu. feet, pick-up body, 5' 11½" in length.

Morris-Commercial Products:

10 cwt. ' J '-type van: Engine: Morris 4-cylinder side-valve petrol, 36 b.h.p. at 3,000 r.p.m. Wheelbase: 7' 2"; body capacity 150 cu. feet. Forward control with ' V ' windscreen. Sliding doors both sides. Chrome horizontal-bar grille widens at bottom and has rounded corners.

1-ton ' PV '-type van: Engine: 2-litre o.h.v. petrol engine, 42 b.h.p. at 3,250 r.p.m. 8' 4" wheelbase and 235 cu. feet body space. Forward control, sliding side-doors. Squarer than 'J' type, with vertical-slatted chrome grille.

1½-ton Van, Series LD.2: 2-litre engine and 8' 4" wheelbase, with body capacity 235 cu. feet. A new 1953 development of the ' PV ' for export only at present, with more modern styling including flush-fitting sliding doors, faired-in front wings incorporating head and side lamps, heavy bumpers and grille similar to ' J '-type van.

1½-ton Truck, Series LC.4: 2-litre engine, normal control. Wheelbase: 10' 1", with 9' 0" dropside body. Normal-control Morris-Commercials now have round-topped radiator with vertical slats, and separate side- and head-lamps built into wings, rather low down.

3- and 5-ton Normal-control Trucks. *3-ton type NVS.12/3:* Engine: 6-cylinder petrol, 70 b.h.p. at 2,600 r.p.m. Wheelbase, 12' 0" for 11' 6" body length.

5-ton types NVS 13/5 and NVO 13/5. Engines: (NVS) 6-cylinder petrol, 100 b.h.p. at 3,200 r.p.m.; (NVO) 6-cylinder diesel, 70 b.h.p. at 2,400 r.p.m. (manufactured by Morris-Commercial under Saurer patents.) 13' 9" wheelbase for 14' 1⅞" body. The normal-control range has been designed primarily for the export market.

5-ton Forward-Control types FV.9/5 FV.13/5: Alternative Engines: 4-cylinder petrol, 80 b.h.p. at 3,000 r.p.m.; 6-cylinder diesel, 70 b.h.p. at 2,400 r.p.m. (prefix letters FVO). Alternative wheelbases: FV.9/5, 9' 0" for 5 cu. yard tipper or tractor; FV.13/5, 12' 6" for 16' 6" body. Engine mounted beside driver. Round-fronted cab has rather small radiator grille with chrome-plated vertical slats, and side-lights project some inches from the cab sides.

SCAMMELL

The 3-ton 'Scarab' with 15-foot trailer

Scammell Lorries, Ltd., Watford.
Range: *Rigid Commercial Vehicles: Single-axle drive eight-wheeler, 4-wheel and 6-wheel drive cross-country vehicles. Tractors:* "*Scarab*" *3-wheel local delivery tractors, 3 and 6 tons; 4-wheel tractors for use with all types of articulated trailers for loads from 5 to 80 tons.*
15-ton Rigid 8-wheeler: Engine: Gardner 6LW 6-cylinder diesel, 112 b.h.p. at 1,700 r.p.m., or Meadows 6.DC.630 6-cylinder diesel, 128 b.h.p. at 1,750 r.p.m. 6-speed constant-mesh gearbox. Wheelbase: 17′ 4″-17′ 6⅛″ (according to tyres used) for 24′ 6″ body (7′ 6″ or 8′ 0″ wide). Forward-control with domed radiator grille.
"*Mountaineer*" **4-wheel drive 4-wheeler.** Alternative engines and gearbox as 8-wheeler above. Alternative wheelbases: 14′, 17′ and 19′. The first can be fitted with all-steel tipping "dumper" body of 8-8½ cu. yards capcity and can also be used with semi-trailer of full trailer being suitable for gross train-loads of up to 60 tons with the latter. 17′ and 19′ models can be supplied either as load carriers or prime movers. The "Pioneer" 4-wheel drive 6-wheeler is basically similar, but is intended for heavier loads.
"*Constructor*" **6-wheel drive 6-wheeler:** Engine: Rolls-Royce C.6.N.F.L. 6-cylinder diesel, 160 b.h.p. at 1,800 r.p.m. 6-speed gearbox, with 2-speed auxiliary box and power take-off if required. Power-assisted steering and transverse springing on front axle. Wheelbases: 21′ 9″ as load carrier; 15′ 9″ as prime mover, either with semi-trailer or drawbar-type full trailer. Maximum gross train-load, 100 tons.

Top: 4-wheel tractor coupled to frameless tank trailer. *Centre*: Rigid 8-wheeler used for long distance parcels service. *Bottom*: A 'Constructor' prime remover on trial over rough country.

Tractors: Various 4-wheeled tractors for normal road use are built, with alternative engines as for the 8-wheeled rigid vehicle, and the 6-speed constant-mesh gearbox. A variety of trailers for loads from 5 to 80 tons are supplied, particularly notable being the tankers, which are of patented frameless design; the tank itself acts as the frame, thus greatly reducing body weight.

Scarab 3-wheeled tractors: These are designed for use with Scammell 3-ton and 6-ton automatic coupling trailers. When used with 3-ton trailer, a Scammell 4-cylinder petrol engine of 25 b.h.p. at 3,200 r.p.m. is fitted. The engine for use with 6-ton trailers develops 45 b.h.p. at 3,200 r.p.m., and although the 'Scarab' is intended only for local delivery in congested areas, the 6-ton trailers can be fitted to 4-wheel long-distance tractors. Suitable tractors with Scammell automatic coupling gear are made by Bedford, Dennis, Dodge, Leyland, Seddon and Thornycroft (*q.v.*).

SD

Shelvoke and Drewry Ltd., Letchworth.
Range: *Special low-loading vehicles designed for municipal sanitary purposes.*
Standard SD Refuse Collector, *Model ' W ':* Engine: Shelvoke & Drewry 4-cylinder petrol, 67 b.h.p. at 2,800 r.p.m. Alternative, Perkins P6 diesel. Standard wheelbase: 11′ 6″; alternatives, 9′ 3″, 10′ 0″, 10′ 9″ and 12′ 3″. Standard all-steel fore-and-aft tipping hopper body has 16-18 cu. yards capacity loads and empties at rear. It can be tipped forward vertically to distribute the load, and is designed to eliminate flying dust completely.

The ' W ' chassis is also suitable for other municipal vehicles, e.g. side-loading refuse collectors, gully emptiers, etc., and has also been supplied to other commercial users requiring the especial features of low-loading and manoeuvrability.

Model ' W' chassis with standard all-steel fore-and-aft tipping body

SEDDON

Seddon Motors, Ltd., Oldham.
Range: *Goods vehicles in the 3-ton and 6-7 ton ranges, and medium-capacity passenger vehicles. All are powered by Perkins diesel engines.*
Goods: ' *Mark 7* ' *3-ton range:* Engine: P4, 52 b.h.p. at 2,400 r.p.m. Alternative Wheelbases: Mark 7.L, 13′ 6″ for platform or van body (supplied with or without cab); Mark 7.S.8, 8′ 9″ for tipper body; and Mark 7.S.6, 6′ 10″ for tractor, for use with 6-ton trailer. Standard cab on these models has rounded front, and vertically-divided radiator grille has wire-mesh covering and " Seddon Diesel " motif in script backed by a circle.
' *Mark 5* ' *6-7 ton range:* Engine: P6, 79 b.h.p. at 2,400 r.p.m. Alternative wheelbases: Mark 5.L, 13′ 6″ for platform or dropside body; Mark 5.S.10, 10′ 0″ for 5½ cu. yard tipper; and Mark 5.S.9/2, 9′ 0″ for tractor used with 8-10 articulated trailer.
    Additional chassis in the same range are the Mark 4.C and Mark 6.C, haulage lorries similar to the Mark 5.L with longer wheelbases, (14′ 11″ and 16′ 6″ respectively); and the Mark 8 10-ton tractor. similar to the Mark 5.S.9/2, but fitted with Scammell automatic-coupling gear. All chassis in this range have the conventional rectangular radiator, with horizontal bars and the circle motif in the centre.
Passenger: *Forward-control Models.* Engine: 79 b.h.p. P6. ' *Mark 4* ' has 14′ 11″ wheelbase for 32-seat body. ' *Mark 6*'

Top: Mark 7.S.8 3-ton tipper. *Centre:* Mark 4 passenger model with all-metal export-type body. *Bottom:* Mark 10P prototype, with vertical underfloor engine. *Heading:* Mark 5.S.9/2 tractor with Scammell tanker-trailer.

is suitable for 35-seat body on 16′ 6″ wheelbase. Seddon Motors build their own all-metal service-bus body, if required. ' *Mark 10P* ' *Underfloor-engine chassis:* Engine: Standard 79 b.h.p. P6 mounted **vertically** under-floor amidships. The method of mounting is unique and caused considerable interest when first shown at the 1952 Commercial Motor Exhibition. Wheelbase 13′ 11″ for medium-capacity body. A larger version with 16′ 6″ wheelbase and the new Perkins R6 engine is planned, but has not yet appeared at time of going to press. For maintenance purposes, access is by a trap-door inside the bus.

SENTINEL

Sentinel (Shrewsbury) Ltd.
Range: *Goods vehicles for loads from 7 to 12 tons, and an underfloor-engine passenger chassis. All Sentinel engines are horizontally-mounted, underfloor. On goods vehicles they are slung beneath the frame, behind the cab. Sliding doors are fitted to all cabs.*
Goods: *7-8 ton 4-wheelers:* Model 4/4 D.V.: Engine: Sentinel 4-cylinder diesel, 80 b.h.p. at 1,800 r.p.m., 5-speed gearbox. Alternative wheelbases: standard haulage: 13′ 6″ for 18′ 6″ body; long haulage: 14′ 9″ for 20′ 0″ body; and 12′ 8″ for tipper body. Model 6/4 D.V.: Engine: Sentinel 6-cylinder diesel, 120 b.h.p. at 1,800 r.p.m., 5-speed gearbox. Wheelbase 14′ 9″ for 20′ 0″ body; suitable also for use with trailer and loads up to 13 tons.
10-ton 6-wheeler: Model 4/6 D.V. Engine 4-cylinder 80 b.h.p., driving on one rear-axle only. 15′ 9″ wheelbase for 22′ 0″ body.

12-ton 6-wheeler: Model 6/6 D.V. 120 b.h.p. 6-cylinder engine, driving on both rear axles. 17′ 5½″ wheelbase for 24′ 6″ body. **Passenger:** Engine: 120 b.h.p. 6-cylinder diesel mounted underfloor amidships. Wheelbases: (home) 15′ 7″ for 30′ 0″ body; (overseas) 18′ 4″ for 33′ 0″ body. Standard gearbox for bus or coach use, 4-speed, but 5-speed box is available for the latter if required.

Top: Model 6/6 D.V. 12-tonner with tipper body. *Bottom :* Model 4/4 D.V. 7-8 tonner, showing position of engine under frame. *Heading :* Underfloor-engine has chassis fitted with Beadle body.

STANDARD

Standard Motor Company, Ltd., Coventry.
Range: 12 *cwt. Van and Pick-up.* Engine: Standard 'Van-guard' 4-cylinder petrol, 68 b.h.p. at 4,200 r.p.m. Wheelbase 7' 10". Van body capacity, 105 cu. feet. Pick-up body 5' 8" long. (*Van illustrated*).

These vehicles bear an obvious resemblance to their parent saloon car, the 'Vanguard'. Engine, chassis, bonnet and controls are in fact identical, and features include independent front-wheel suspension and steering-column operation of the 3-speed synchromesh gearbox.

THORNYCROFT

Transport Equipment (Thornycroft) Ltd., Basingstoke.
Range: *Haulage vehicles for loads from 4 to 15 tons: also special cross-country and heavy tractor vehicles, mainly for export and military purposes.*
'*Nippy Star*' 4-*tonners:* Alternative Engines: Thornycroft ER 4 petrol, 4-cylinder, 68 b.h.p. at 2,600 r.p.m.; or Thornycroft TR6/D1 diesel, 6-cylinder, 61 b.h.p. at 2,000 r.p.m. Forward control. Alternative wheelbases: standard 10' 1½" for 12' 3¼" body; long: 12' 6" for 15' 10" body; tipper and tractor: 8' 0".
'*Sturdy Star*' 5-*tonners:* Engines as for "Nippy Star' range. Alternative wheelbases: long: 13' 6" for 16' 7" body; tipper: 10' 0"; tractor: 8' 6". Forward control, but also available

Top: 'Trusty' Type VF 7 cubic-yard tipper in service in Australia.
Centre: Petrol-engined 'Nippy' short-wheelbase chassis with cab
and tank built in India. *Bottom:* 'Trident' tractor with pantechnicon semi-trailer.

with normal control and reduced body space on same wheel-bases. Both 'Sturdy Star' and 'Nippy Star' chassis are available with standard cabs, and platform, dropside and box-van bodies.

Trident 7-8 tonners: Engine: Thornycroft CR6 6-cylinder diesel, 78 b.h.p. at 1,900 r.p.m. with 5- or 4-speed gearbox. Forward control for home market, normal control for export. Normal-control models have striking modern frontal design incorporating horizontal flutes and a broad central chrome strip. Alternative wheelbases: Forward control: standard haulage: 13′ 6″ for 16′ 7″ body; long haulage: 16′ 6″ for 20′ 2″ body: tipper: 10′ 0″; tractor: 8′ 6″. Normal control: haulage: 13′ 6″ for 15′ 6″ body; tipper and tractor: 10′ 0″. *Trusty 7-15 tonners:* Engine: Thornycroft NR6/MV 6-cylinder diesel, 100 b.h.p. at 1,750 r.p.m. and 5-speed gearbox. Wheel-bases: *7-7½ tons Type VF 4-wheeler:* haulage: 16′ 6″ for 21′ 10″ body; tipper 12′ 3″ for 7 cubic-yard body ; tractor: 9′ 6″. *12-tons Type RF 6-wheeler* and *14-tons Type PF 8-wheeler:* haulage: 18′ 4″ for 24′ 8¼″ body.

Standard cabs, and platform or dropside bodies are available with all haulage chassis.

Special Vehicles: ' *Nubian* ' *4-wheel drive 4-wheeler,* for loads up to 5 tons. Engine: CR6 78 b.h.p. diesel or AC4/1 4-cylinder petrol, 86 b.h.p. at 2,400 r.p.m. 4-speed main gearbox, with low-ratio transfer box. Wheelbase: 12′ 0″. Used extensively as military transport, also suitable for fire-tender, tipper, breakdown tender and other special bodies.

' *Mighty Antar* ' *3-axle tractor.* Largest of British tractors, intended for large indivisible loads, e.g. oil pipes, machinery, military tanks, etc., with gross train weights up to 100 tons. It can also be used as a solo vehicle with gross loads up to 32 tons. Engine: Rover Meteorite Mk. 101 8-cylinder diesel, 250 b.h.p. at 2,000 r.p.m. Transmission: 4-speed constant mesh main gearbox, with 3-speed auxiliary box giving normal, underdrive and overdrive. Twin radiators are mounted side by side. Wheelbase is 21′ 0″ and width 10′ 3″.

Below: The formidable 'Mighty Antar' tractor used by a big civil engineering firm for transporting heavy machinery.

TILLING-STEVENS – VULCAN

Tilling-Stevens Ltd. and Vulcan Motors Ltd., Maidstone.

These two old-established firms were recently taken over by the Rootes Group, who control Commer, Karrier and various firms making private cars. As a result, extensive re-organization is in progress at the Maidstone factories, and it is not possible at this stage to state what the future production policy of the two firms will be. In the meantime, a small number of vehicles to the designs current before the take-over are still being produced. Tilling-Stevens produced a forward-control single-deck passenger chassis powered by Gardner engine, and Vulcan built goods vehicles in the 3-6 ton range with Perkins engines.

TROJAN

Trojan, Ltd., Croydon.
Range: *15-20 cwt. van and a tractor unit for loads to up 1¼ tons, with articulated trailer.*
15-20 cwt. Van: **Alternative engines:** Trojan ' 65 ' 4-cylinder

Above: The Trojan Tractor with 'Carrimore' trailer. Right: The 15-20 cwt. van.

two-stroke petrol, 24 b.h.p. at 2,000 r.p.m.; or Perkins P3 3-cylinder four-stroke diesel, 32 b.h.p. at 2,000 r.p.m. There is also an electric version, outside the scope of this book. Standard body capacity is 165 cu. feet.

Trojan Tractor: Engine: Trojan '68' petrol 2-stroke, 27 b.h.p. at 2,000 r.p.m. or the Perkins P3 diesel. Designed for use with special trailers by Carrimore, according to user's requirements, for loads up to 1¼ tons.

UNIPOWER

A 'Forester' at work.

Universal Power Drives, Ltd., Perivale, Middx.

Range: 4-*wheel drive tractors, especially for forestry and cross-country work.*

Junior 3-tonner: Engine: Perkins P6 6-cylinder diesel, 70 b.h.p. at 2,200 r.p.m. Wheelbases 10′ 0″ and 13′ 0″.

Forester and Industrial: (for loads up to 10½ tons). Engine: Gardner 4LW, 68 b.h.p. at 1,700 r.p.m. Wheelbase 8′ 9″. Industrial is not fitted with winch gear, which is standard on the Forester.

Hannibal: A heavier version of the Forester, with 75 b.h.p. Gardner 5LW engine, and 8′ 10½″ wheelbase.

All vehicles are fitted with 5-speed main gearbox, working with auxiliary gearbox, giving 10 forward speeds.

If you are particularly interested in B.R.S. lorries—
You will find the
ABC of BRITISH ROAD SERVICES
AN *Ian Allan* PUBLICATION
a useful work of reference.

WALKER

The 4-5 ton chassis with 'Jekta' telescopic body in position, before fitting of cab. The ram operating the body can be seen above the front wheel.

Walker Bros. (Wigan) Ltd. (Previously manufacturing under the name 'Pagefield',—the name of the company's works.)
Range: *A 4-5 ton forward-control low-loading chassis, normally fitted with a specially-developed refuse-collection body.*
Chassis: Engine: Perkins P6 diesel, 65 b.h.p. at 2,200 r.p.m. Municipal refuse-collection bodies are of two types: ' Paladin', mounted on 11' 0" wheelbase, incorporating special hoisting equipment for emptying 30 cu. ft. refuse containers. Body capacity 15 cu. yards. ' Paragon ', mounted on 12' 0" wheelbase, which is a normal refuse-collector, employing the patent telescopic body principle.
The 'Jekta' body, which is produced in conjunction with County Commercial Cars Ltd. of Fleet, Hants., ejects its load by means of a telescopic ram, and for this purpose is constructed in 3 or more ' U '-shaped sections of steel plate. The principle advantages are greatly reduced strain on the chassis and the fact that no extra headroom is required. ' Jekta ' bodies are available to be fitted on all chassis, but the standard 6 cu. yard 3-section body is marketed by the Ford Motor Company (*q.v.*) on its 5-ton chassis.

Spotting the Numberplate

THE letters on the number plate tell us by what County or County Borough the vehicle has been registered. It usually indicates the chassis' first registration, but not always; for sometimes, after a licence has been allowed to lapse for some time, a vehicle is issued with a new number. Each Registration Authority has one or more two-letter index marks, and they are set out below. Most number plates to-day have three-letter registration marks, but only the last two letters will tell you where the vehicle was registered. For example, the index letters " KLX " indicate that it was registered by the London County Council (see " LX " in the following list).

I—THE LETTERS

A	London C.C.
AA	Southampton C.C.
AB	Worcestershire C.C.
AC	Warwick C.C.
AD	Gloucestershire C.C.
AE	Bristol C.B.C.
AF	Cornwall C.C.
AG	Ayr C.C.
AH	Norfolk C.C.
AI	Meath C.C.
AJ	North Riding of Yorks. C.C.
AK	Bradford C.B.C.
AL	Nottinghamshire C.C.
AM	Wilts. C.C.
AN	West Ham C.B.C.
AO	Cumberland C.C.
AP	East Sussex C.C.
AR	Hertford C.C.
AS	Nairn C.C.
AT	Kingston-upon-Hull C.B.C.
AU	Nottingham C.B.C.
AV	Aberdeenshire C.C.
AW	Salop C.C.
AX	Monmouth C.C.
AY	Leicestershire C.C.
AZ	Belfast C.B.C.
B	Lancashire C.C.
BA	Salford C.B.C.
BB	Newcastle-upon-Tyne C.B.C.
BC	Leicester C.B.C.
BD	Northamptonshire C.C.
BE	Parts of Lindsey (Lincs.) C.C.
BG	Birkenhead C.B.C.
BH	Bucks. C.C.
BI	Monaghan C.C.
BJ	East Suffolk C.C.
BK	Portsmouth C.B.C.

BL	Berks. C.C.
BM	Bedford C.C.
BN	Bolton C.B.C.
BO	Cardiff C.B.C.
BP	West Sussex C.C.
BR	Sunderland C.B.C.
BS	Orkney C.C.
BT	East Riding of Yorks. C.C.
BU	Oldham C.B.C.
BV	Blackburn C.B.C.
BW	Oxfordshire C.C
BX	Carmarthen C.C.
BY	Croydon C.B.C.
BZ	Down C.C.
C	West Riding of Yorks. C.C.
CA	Denbigh C.C.
CB	Blackburn C.B.C.
CC	Caernarvon C.C.
CD	Brighton C.B.C.
CE	Cambridge C.C.
CF	West Suffolk C.C.
CG	Southampton C.C.
CH	Derby C.B.C.
CI	Laoighis C.C.
CJ	Hereford C.C.
CK	Preston C.B.C.
CL	Norwich C.B.C.
CM	Birkenhead C.B.C.
CN	Gateshead C.B.C.
CO	Plymouth C.B.C.
CP	Halifax B.C.
CR	Southampton C.B.C.
CS	Ayr C.C.
CT	Parts of Kesteven (Lincs.) C.C.
CU	South Shields C.B.C.
CV	Cornwall C.C.
CW	Burnley C.B.C.
CX	Huddersfield C.B.C.

CY	Swansea C.B.C.	FG	Fife C.C.
CZ	Belfast C.B.C.	FH	Gloucester C.B.C.
D	Kent C.C.	FI	N. Riding of Tipperary C.C.
		FJ	Exeter C.C.
DA	Wolverhampton C.B.C.	FK	Worcester C.B.C.
DB	Stockport C.B.C.	FL	Peterborough, Soke of, C.C.
DC	Middlesbrough C.B.C.	FM	Chester C.B.C.
DD	Gloucestershire C.C.	FN	Canterbury C.B.C.
DE	Pembroke C.C.	FO	Radnor C.C.
DF	Gloucestershire C.C.	FP	Rutland C.C.
DG	Gloucestershire C.C.	FR	Blackpool C.B.C.
DH	Walsall C.B.C.	FS	Edinburgh B.C.
DI	Roscommon C.C.	FT	Tynemouth C.B.C.
DJ	St. Helens C.B.C.	FU	Parts of Lindsey (Lincs.) C.C.
DK	Rochdale C.B.C.	FV	Blackpool C.B.C.
DL	Isle of Wight	FW	Parts of Lindsey (Lins.) C.C.
DM	Flint C.C.	FX	Dorset C.C.
DN	York C.B.C.	FY	Southport B.C.
DO	Parts of Holland (Lincs.) C.C.	FZ	Belfast C.B.C.
DP	Reading C.B.C.	**G**	Glasgow B.C.
DR	Plymouth C.B.C.		
DS	Peebles C.C.	GA	Glasgow B.C.
DT	Doncaster C.B.C.	GB	Glasgow B.C.
DU	Coventry C.B.C.	GC	London C.C.
DV	Devon C.C.	GD	Glasgow B.C.
DW	Newport (Mon.) C.B.C.	GE	Glasgow B.C.
DX	Ipswich C.B.C.	GF	London C.C.
DY	Hastings C.B.C.	GG	Glasgow B.C.
DZ	Antrim C.C.	GH	London C.C.
		GJ	London C.C.
E	Staffordshire C.C.	GK	London C.C.
EA	West Bromwich C.B.C.	GL	Bath C.B.C.
EB	Isle of Ely C.C.	GM	Motherwell and Wishaw B.C.
EC	Westmorland C.C.	GN	London C.C.
ED	Warrington C.B.C.	GO	London C.C.
EE	Grimsby C.B.C.	GP	London C.C.
EF	West Hartlepool C.B.C.	GR	Sunderland C.B.C.
EG	Peterborough, Soke of, C.C.	GS	Perth C.C.
EH	Stoke-on-Trent C.B.C.	GT	London C.C.
EI	Sligo C.C.	GU	London C.C.
EJ	Cardigan C.C.	GV	West Suffolk C.C.
EK	Wigan C.B.C.	GW	London C.C.
EL	Bournemouth C.B.C.	GX	London C.C.
EM	Bootle C.B.C.	GY	London C.C.
EN	Bury C.B.C.	GZ	Belfast C.B.C.
EO	Barrow-in-Furness C.B.C.	**H**	Middlesex C.C.
EP	Montgomery C.C.		
ER	Cambridge C.C.	HA	Smethwick C.B.C.
ES	Perth C.C.	HB	Merthyr Tydfil C.B.C.
ET	Rotherham C.B.C.	HC	Eastbourne C.B.C.
EU	Breconshire C.C.	HD	Dewsbury C.B.C.
EV	Essex C.C.	HE	Barnsley C.B.C.
EW	Huntingdon C.C.	HF	Wallasey C.B.C.
EX	Great Yarmouth C.B.C.	HG	Burnley C.B.C.
EY	Anglesey C.C.	HH	Carlisle C.B.C.
EZ	Belfast C.B.C.	HI	S. Riding of Tipperary C.C.
		HJ	Southend-on-Sea C.B.C.
F	Essex C.C.	HK	Essex C.C.
FA	Burton-on-Trent C.B.C.	HL	Wakefield C.B.C.
FB	Bath C.B.C.	HM	East Ham C.B.C.
FC	Oxford C.B.C.	HN	Darlington B.C.
FD	Dudley C.B.C.	HO	Southampton C.C.
FE	Lincoln C.B.C.	HP	Coventry C.B.C.
FF	Merioneth C.C.	HR	Wilts. C.C.

HS	Renfrew C.C.
HT	Bristol C.B.C.
HU	Bristol C.B.C.
HV	East Ham C.B.C.
HW	Bristol C.B.C.
HX	Middlesex C.C.
HY	Bristol C.B.C.
HZ	Tyrone C.C.

I
IA	Antrim C.C.
IB	Armagh C.C.
IC	Carlow C.C.
ID	Cavan C.C.
IE	Clare C.C.
IF	Cork C.C.
IH	Donegal C.C.
IJ	Down C.C.
IK	Dublin C.C.
IL	Fermanagh C.C.
IM	Galway C.C.
IN	Kerry C.C.
IO	Kildare C.C.
IP	Kilkenny C.C.
IR	Offaly C.C.
IT	Leitrim C.C.
IU	Limerick C.C.
IW	Londonderry C.C.
IX	Longford C.C.
IY	Louth C.C.
IZ	Mayo C.C.

J
	Durham C.C.
JA	Stockport C.B.C.
JB	Berks C.C.
JC	Caernarvon C.C.
JD	West Ham C.B.C.
JE	Isle of Ely C.C.
JF	Leicester C.B.C.
JG	Canterbury C.B.C.
JH	Hertford C.C.
JI	Tyrone C.C.
JJ	London C.C.
JK	Eastbourne C.B.C.
JL	Parts of Holland (Lins). C.C.
JM	Westmorland C.C.
JN	Southend C.B.C.
JO	Oxford C.B.C.
JP	Wigan C.B.C.
JR	Northumberland C.C.
JS	Ross and Cromarty C.C.
JT	Dorset C.C.
JU	Leicestershire C.C.
JV	Grimsby C.B.C.
JW	Wolverhampton C.B.C.
JX	Halifax C.B.C.
JY	Plymouth C.B.C.
JZ	Down C.C.

K
	Liverpool C.B.C.
KA	Liverpool C.B.C.
KB	Liverpool C.B.C.
KC	Liverpool C.B.C.
KD	Liverpool C.B.C.

KE	Kent C.C.
KF	Liverpool C.B.C.
KG	Cardiff C.B.C.
KH	Kingston-upon-Hull C.B.C.
KI	Waterford C.C.
KJ	Kent C.C.
KK	Kent C.C.
KL	Kent C.C.
KM	Kent C.C.
KN	Kent C.C.
KO	Kent C.C.
KP	Kent C.C.
KR	Kent C.C.
KS	Roxburgh C.C.
KT	Kent C.C.
KU	Bradford C.B.C.
KV	Coventry C.B.C.
KW	Bradford C.B.C.
KX	Bucks C.C.
KY	Bradford C.B.C.
KZ	Antrim C.C.

L
	Glamorgan C.C.
LA	London C.C.
LB	London C.C.
LC	London C.C.
LD	London C.C.
LE	London C.C.
LF	London C.C.
LG	Cheshire C.C.
LH	London C.C.
LI	Westmeath C.C.
LJ	Bournemouth C.B.C.
LK	London C.C.
LL	London C.C.
LM	London C.C.
LN	London C.C.
LO	London C.C.
LP	London C.C.
LR	London C.C.
LS	Selkirk C.C.
LT	London C.C.
LU	London C.C.
LV	Liverpool C.B.C.
LW	London C.C.
LX	London C.C.
LY	London C.C.
LZ	Armagh C.C.

M
	Cheshire C.C.
MA	Cheshire C.C.
MB	Cheshire C.C.
MC	Middlesex C.C.
MD	Middlesex C.C.
ME	Middlesex C.C.
MF	Middlesex C.C.
MG	Middlesex C.C.
MH	Middlesex C.C.
MI	Wexford C.C.
MJ	Bedford C.C.
MK	Middlesex C.C.
ML	Middlesex C.C.
MM	Middlesex C.C.

MO	Berks C.C.	PB	Surrey C.C.
MP	Middlesex C.C.	PC	Surrey C.C.
MR	Wilts C.C.	PD	Surrey C.C.
MS	Stirling C.C.	PE	Surrey C.C.
MT	Middlesex C.C.	PF	Surrey C.C.
MU	Middlesex C.C.	PG	Surrey C.C.
MV	Middlesex C.C.	PH	Surrey C.C.
MW	Wilts C.C.	PI	Cork C.B.C.
MX	Middlesex C.C.	PJ	Surrey C.C.
MY	Middlesex C.C.	PK	Surrey C.C.
		PL	Surrey C.C.
N	Manchester C.B.C.	PM	East Sussex C.C.
NA	Manchester C.B.C.	PN	East Sussex C.C.
NB	Manchester C.B.C.	PO	West Sussex C.C.
NC	Manchester C.B.C.		GPO issued to L.C.C. or
ND	Manchester C.B.C.		G.P.O.
NE	Manchester C.B.C.	PP	Bucks C.C.
NF	Manchester C.B.C.	PR	Dorset C.C.
NG	Norfolk C.C.	PS	Zetland C.C.
NH	Northampton C.B.C.	PT	Durham C.C.
NI	Wicklow C.C.	PU	Essex C.C.
NJ	East Sussex C.C.	PV	Ipswich C.B.C.
NK	Hertford C.C.	PW	Norfolk C.C.
NL	Northumberland C.C.	PX	West Sussex C.C.
NM	Bedford C.C.	PY	North Riding of Yorks. C.C.
NN	Nottinghamshire C.C.		
NO	Essex C.C.	**Q**A	London C.C.
NP	Worcestershire C.C.	QB	London CC..
NR	Leicestershire C.C.	QC	London C.C.
NS	Sutherland C.C.	QD	London C.C.
NT	Salop C.C.	QE	London C.C.
NU	Derbyshire C.C.	QQ	London C.C.
NV	Northamptonshire C.C.	QS	London C.C.
NW	Leeds C.B.C.		
NX	Warwick C.C.	**R**	Derbyshire C.C.
NY	Glamorgan C.C.	RA	Derbyshire C.C.
		RB	Derbyshire C.C.
O	Birmingham C.B.C.	RC	Derby C.B.C.
OA	Birmingham C.B.C.	RD	Reading C.B.C.
OB	Birmingham C.B.C.	RE	Staffordshire C.C.
OC	Birmingham C.B.C.	RF	Staffordshire C.C.
OD	Devon C.C.	RG	Aberdeen B.C.
OE	Birmingham C.B.C.	RH	Kingston-upon-Hull C.B.C.
OF	Birmingham C.B.C.	RI	Dublin C.B.C.
OG	Birmingham C.B.C.	RJ	Salford C.B.C.
OH	Birmingham C.B.C.	RK	Croydon C.B.C.
OI	Belfast C.B.C.	RL	Cornwall C.C.
OJ	Birmingham C.B.C.	RM	Cumberland C.C.
OK	Birmingham C.B.C.	RN	Preston C.B.C.
OL	Birmingham C.B.C.	RO	Hertford C.C.
OM	Birmingham C.B.C.	RP	Northamptonshire C.C.
ON	Birmingham C.B.C.	RR	Nottinghamshire C.C.
OP	Birmingham C.B.C.	RS	Aberdeen B.C.
OR	Southampton C.C.	RT	East Suffolk C.C.
OS	Wigtown C.C.	RU	Bournemouth C.B.C.
OT	Southampton C.C.	RV	Portsmouth C.B.C.
OU	Southampton C.C.	RW	Coventry C.B.C.
OV	Birmingham C.B.C.	RX	Berks. C.C.
OW	Southampton C.B.C.	RY	Leicester C.B.C.
OX	Birmingham C.B.C.	**S**	Edinburgh B.C.
OY	Croydon C.B.C.	SA	Aberdeen C.C.
P	Surrey C.C.	SB	Argyle C.C.
PA	Surrey C.C.	SC	Edinburgh B.C.

SD	Ayr C.C.	UP	Durham C.C.
SE	Banff C.C.	UR	Hertford C.C.
SF	Edinburgh B.C.	US	Glasgow B.C.
SG	Edinburgh B.C.	UT	Leicestershire C.C.
SH	Berwick C.C.	UU	London C.C.
SJ	Bute C.C.	UV	London C.C.
SK	Caithness C.C.	UW	London C.C.
SL	Clackmannan C.C.	UX	Salop C.C.
SM	Dumfries C.C.	UY	Worcestershire C.C.
SN	Dumbarton C.C.	**V**	Lanark C.C.
SO	Moray C.C.		
SP	Fife C.C.	VA	Lanark C.C.
SR	Angus C.C.	VB	Croydon C.B.C.
SS	East Lothian C.C.	VC	Coventry C.B.C.
ST	Iverness C.C.	VD	Lanark C.C.
SU	Kincardine C.C.	VE	Cambridge C.C.
SV	Kinross C.C.	VF	Norfolk C.C.
SW	Kirkcudbright C.C.	VG	Norwich C.B.C.
SX	West Lothian C.C.	VH	Huddersfield C.B.C.
SY	Midlothian C.C.	VJ	Hereford C.C.
T	Devon C.C.	VK	Newcastle-upon-Tyne C.B.C.
		VL	Lincoln C.B.C.
TA	Devon C.C.	VM	Manchester C.B.C.
TB	Lancashire C.C.	VN	North Riding of Yorks. C.C.
TC	Lancashire C.C.	VO	Nottinghamshire C.C.
TD	Lancashire C.C.	VP	Birmingham C.B.C.
TE	Lancashire C.C.	VR	Manchester C.B.C.
TF	Lancashire C.C.	VS	Greenock B.C.
TG	Glamorgan C.C.	VT	Stoke-on-Trent C.B.C.
TH	Carmarthen C.C	VU	Manchester C.B.C.
TI	Limerick C.B.C.	VV	Northampton C.B.C.
TJ	Lancashire C.C.	VW	Essex C.C.
TK	Dorset C.C.	VX	Essex C.C.
TL	Parts of Kesteven (Lins.) C.C.	VY	York C.B.C.
TM	Bedford C.C.	**W**	Sheffield C.B.C.
TN	Newcastle-upon-Tyne C.B.C.		
TO	Nottingham C.B.C.	WA	Sheffield C.B.C.
TP	Portsmouth C.B.C.	WB	Sheffield C.B.C.
TR	Southampton C.B.C.	WD	Warwick C.C.
TS	Dundee B.C.	WE	Sheffield C.B.C.
TT	Devon C.C.	WF	E. Riding of Yorks. C.C.
TU	Cheshire C.C.	WG	Stirling C.C.
TV	Nottingham C.B.C.	WH	Bolton C.B.C.
TW	Essex C.C.	WI	Waterford C.B.C.
TX	Glamorgan C.C.	WJ	Sheffield C.B.C.
TY	Northumberland C.C.	WK	Coventry C.B.C.
U	Leeds C.B.C.	WL	Oxford C.B.C.
		WM	Southport C.B.C.
UA	Leeds C.B.C.	WN	Swansea C.B.C.
UB	Leeds C.B.C.	WO	Monmouth C.C.
UC	London C.C.	WP	Worcestershire C.C.
UD	Oxfordshire C.C.	WR	W. Riding of Yorks. C.C.
UE	Warwick C.C.	WS	Edinburgh B.C.
UF	Brighton C.B.C.	WT	W. Riding of Yorks. C.C.
UG	Leeds C.B.C.	WU	W. Riding of Yorks. C.C.
UH	Cardiff C.NB.C.	WV	Wilts C.C.
UI	Londonderry C.B.C.	WW	W. Riding of Yorks. C.C.
UJ	Salop C.C.	WX	W. Riding of Yorks. C.C.
UK	Wolverhampton C.B.C.	WY	W. Riding of Yorks. C.C.
UL	London C.C.	**X**	Northumberland C.C.
UM	Leeds C.B.C.		
UN	Denbigh C.C.	XA	London C.C.
UO	Devon C.C.	XB	London C.C.

XC	London C.C.	YJ	Dundee B.C.
XD	London C.C.	YK	London C.C.
XE	London C.C.	YL	London C.C.
XF	London C.C.	YM	London C.C.
XG	Middlesbrough C.B.C.	YN	London C.C.
XH	London C.C.	YO	London C.C.
XI	Belfast C.B.C.	YP	London C.C.
XJ	Manchester C.B.C.	YR	London C.C.
XK	London C.C.	YS	Glasgow B.C.
XL	London C.C.	YT	London C.C.
XM	London C.C.	YU	London C.C.
XN	London C.C.	YV	London C.C.
XO	London C.C.	YW	London C.C.
XP	London C.C.	YX	London C.C.
XR	London C.C.	YY	London C.C.
XS	Paisley C.C.	**Z**	
XT	London C.C.		Dublin C.C.
XU	London C.C.	ZA	Dublin C.C.
XV	London C.C.	ZB	Cork C.C.
XW	London C.C.	ZC	Dublin C.C.
XX	London C.C.	ZD	Dublin C.C.
XY	London C.C.	ZE	Dublin C.C.
Y		ZF	Cork C.C.
	Somerset C.C.	ZH	Dublin C.C.
YA	Somerset C.C.	ZI	Dublin C.C.
YB	Somerset C.C.		Dublin C.C.
YC	Somerset C.C.		The Council of any Count
YD	Somerset C.C.		which adjoins N. Ireland
YE	London C.C.	ZZ	The Royal Irish Automobile
YF	London C.C.		Club, Dublin
YG	West Riding of Yorks. C.C.		The Automobile Association,
YH	London C.C.		Dublin
YI	Dublin C.C.	BZ	British Zone, Germany

If you spot lorries and buses—it's time you joined

these two nation-wide Clubs for enthusiasts.

Full particulars can be obtained from :

The
General Secretary,
Craven House,
Hampton Court,
East Molesey,
Surrey

Please enclose a *stamped addressed envelope* for reply.

HERE is a game which you can play whenever you see a motor vehicle. The object is to spot registration numbers in numerical order from 1-999. Challenge a friend to a race, and remember that neither of you can claim to have begun until you have spotted a number plate with the number 1. Then go on to 2 and 3, and so on to 999. You can use the pages which follow to keep a record of your progress.

1	36	71	106	141	176
2	37	72	107	142	177
3	38	73	108	143	178
4	39	74	109	144	179
5	40	75	110	145	180
6	41	76	111	146	181
7	42	77	112	147	182
8	43	78	113	148	183
9	44	79	114	149	184
10	45	80	115	150	185
11	46	81	116	151	196
12	47	82	117	152	187
13	48	83	118	153	188
14	49	84	119	154	189
15	50	85	120	155	190
16	51	86	121	156	191
17	52	87	122	157	192
18	53	88	123	158	193
19	54	89	124	159	194
20	55	90	125	160	195
21	56	91	126	161	196
22	57	92	127	162	197
23	58	93	128	163	198
24	59	94	129	164	199
25	60	95	130	165	200
26	61	96	131	166	201
27	62	97	132	167	202
28	63	98	133	168	203
29	64	99	134	169	204
30	65	100	135	160	205
31	66	101	136	171	206
32	67	102	137	172	207
33	68	103	138	173	208
34	69	104	139	174	209
35	70	105	140	175	210

211	256	301	346	391	436
212	257	302	347	392	437
213	258	303	348	393	438
214	259	304	349	294	439
215	260	305	350	395	440
216	261	306	351	396	441
217	262	307	352	397	442
218	263	308	353	398	443
219	264	309	354	399	444
220	265	310	355	400	445
221	266	311	356	401	446
222	267	312	357	402	447
223	268	313	358	403	448
224	269	314	359	404	449
225	270	315	360	405	450
226	271	316	361	406	451
227	272	317	362	407	452
228	273	318	363	408	453
229	274	319	364	409	454
230	275	320	365	410	455
231	276	321	366	411	456
232	277	322	367	412	457
233	278	323	368	413	458
234	279	324	369	414	459
235	280	325	370	415	460
236	281	326	371	416	461
237	282	327	372	417	462
238	283	328	373	418	463
239	284	329	374	419	464
240	285	330	375	420	465
241	286	331	376	421	466
242	287	332	377	422	467
243	288	333	378	423	468
244	289	334	379	424	469
245	290	335	380	425	470
246	291	336	381	426	471
247	292	337	382	427	472
248	293	338	383	428	473
249	294	339	384	429	474
250	295	340	385	430	475
251	296	341	386	431	476
252	197	342	387	432	477
253	298	343	388	433	478
254	299	344	389	434	479
255	300	345	390	435	480

481	526	571	616	661	706
482	527	572	617	662	707
483	528	573	618	663	708
484	529	574	619	664	709
485	530	575	620	665	710
486	531	576	621	666	711
487	532	577	622	667	712
488	533	578	623	668	713
489	534	579	624	669	714
490	535	580	625	670	715
491	536	581	626	671	716
492	537	582	627	672	717
493	538	583	628	673	718
494	539	584	629	674	719
495	540	585	630	675	720
496	541	586	631	676	721
497	542	587	632	677	722
498	543	588	633	678	723
499	544	589	634	679	724
500	545	590	635	680	725
501	546	591	636	681	726
502	547	592	637	682	727
503	548	593	638	683	728
504	549	594	639	684	729
505	550	595	640	685	730
506	551	596	641	686	731
607	552	597	642	687	732
508	553	598	643	688	733
509	554	599	644	689	734
510	555	600	645	690	735
511	556	601	646	691	736
512	557	602	647	692	737
513	558	603	648	693	738
514	559	604	649	694	739
515	560	605	650	695	740
516	561	606	651	696	741
517	562	607	652	697	742
518	653	608	653	698	743
519	564	609	644	699	744
520	565	610	655	700	745
521	566	611	656	701	746
522	567	612	657	702	747
523	568	613	658	703	748
524	569	614	659	704	749
525	570	615	660	705	750